JUN 2015

IF YOU WERE A
SNAKE

Clare Hibbert

A+

Smart Apple Media

Published in the United States by Smart Apple Media
PO Box 3263, Mankato, Minnesota 56002

Editor: Joe Harris
Picture researcher: Clare Hibbert
Designer: Emma Randall

Picture credits:
All images Shutterstock unless otherwise specified. FLPA: 5br, 8r, 9b, 10l, 13r, 15 (main), 15 (inset), 17t, 18tr, 25 (inset), 27 (main). NHPA: 17cr.

Library of Congress Cataloging-in-Publication Data

Hibbert, Clare, 1970-
 If you were a snake / Clare Hibbert.
    p. cm. -- (If you were a--)
 Audience: Grade 4 to 6.
 Summary: "Describes the features, life, and habits of snakes, and contrasts them to human life"--Provided by publisher.
 Includes bibliographical references and index.
 ISBN 978-1-59920-963-0 (library binding)
1. Snakes--Juvenile literature. 2. Snakes--Behavior--Juvenile literature. I. Title. II. Title: Snake.
 QL666.O6H588 2014
 597.96--dc23
                                   2013002971

Printed in the United States

Supplier 02, Date 0814, Print Run 2372
SL002679US

98765432

Contents

Seeing and Hearing

If you were a snake, you would be an amazing hunter. However, your senses of sight and hearing would be surprisingly poor. You would be much more reliant on your other senses: taste, smell, and touch.

Hearing without Ears

Snakes don't have ears or eardrums, but they do have a small ear bone inside their skull. Snakes sense sounds as vibrations, not noises. These vibrations, which travel through the air and ground, are carried through the jawbone to the ear bone.

Snake Questions

Q: Can snakes hear music?
A: In India, street entertainers called snake charmers play music that makes snakes "dance". The snakes are not really reacting to the flute playing but to the swaying of the charmers.

Snakes' Eyes

With no eyelids, snakes have a weird, fixed stare. Most snakes are nearsighted (they cannot see far), and what they can see is blurred and unclear. Snakes don't even have muscles to move their eyes.

Sightless Snakes

Blind snakes are just that: blind! They live underground and use other senses to find their favorite food: termites and ant eggs. Blind snakes can wolf down 100 ant eggs a minute!

Supersenses

If you were a snake, you would have highly developed senses of taste and smell and be very sensitive to touch. You might also possess an extraordinary sixth sense: the ability to detect heat. This would be especially useful for hunting in the dead of night.

Heat Seekers

Pythons, boas, and pit vipers have heat pits around their mouth that allow them to detect warm-blooded prey. Pit vipers' brains can turn the information from the pits into an image, so they "see" a thermogram (heat picture) of their prey.

Taste and Smell

Snakes use their flickering tongues both to taste and smell. Their tongues pick up chemicals from the air, then wipe them onto two pits on the roof of the mouth. Those pits are a sense organ called Jacobsen's organ.

Snake Questions

Q: Why do snakes sway their heads?
A: Swaying helps snakes to figure out, using their heat pits, where the strongest heat is coming from—and where their prey is.

Touch
Snakes have receptors all over their bodies that allow them to sense through touch. As they slither along, these receptors give them information about their surroundings.

Hunting Tricks

All 2,700 species of snake are hunters. A few chase down their prey, but most prefer to lie in wait and then ambush it. They rely on excellent camouflage and the ability to remain motionless for hours or even days on end.

Blending In

Snakes that live and hunt among leaf litter often have mottled brown skin, while desert dwellers have sand-colored camouflage. Bright green snakes are hard to spot among lush leaves and vines in tropical rain forests.

Forest Disguise

The leaf-nosed snake lives up in the trees in forests on the island of Madagascar. Its body is the same color as a tree branch, and its nose is shaped like a leaf. This snake catches geckoes and other small lizards to eat.

Snake Questions

Q: How do snakes use their tails to hunt?
A: Some snakes wiggle their tails, luring prey to come within striking distance. The prey thinks the tail is a smaller animal, such as a worm. Sidewinders and eyelash vipers both do this.

Fish Food
The tentacled snake lives in water and has a sneaky trick for catching fish. It holds its head at an angle to its body, then ripples its body toward its prey. The fish, trying to avoid the snake's body, swim right into its waiting jaws!

Constrictors

If you were a snake, you wouldn't want to swallow struggling prey. You'd use venom or constriction to kill your meal first. Constriction means squashing very, very tightly. If you were a constrictor, you'd wrap your body around your victim and squeeze it to death.

Snakes that Squash

Constrictors include the world's biggest snakes—pythons, boa constrictors, and anacondas. The green anaconda grows up to 30 feet (9 m) and weighs up to 550 pounds (227 kg). It eats wild pigs, deer, capybara, even jaguars.

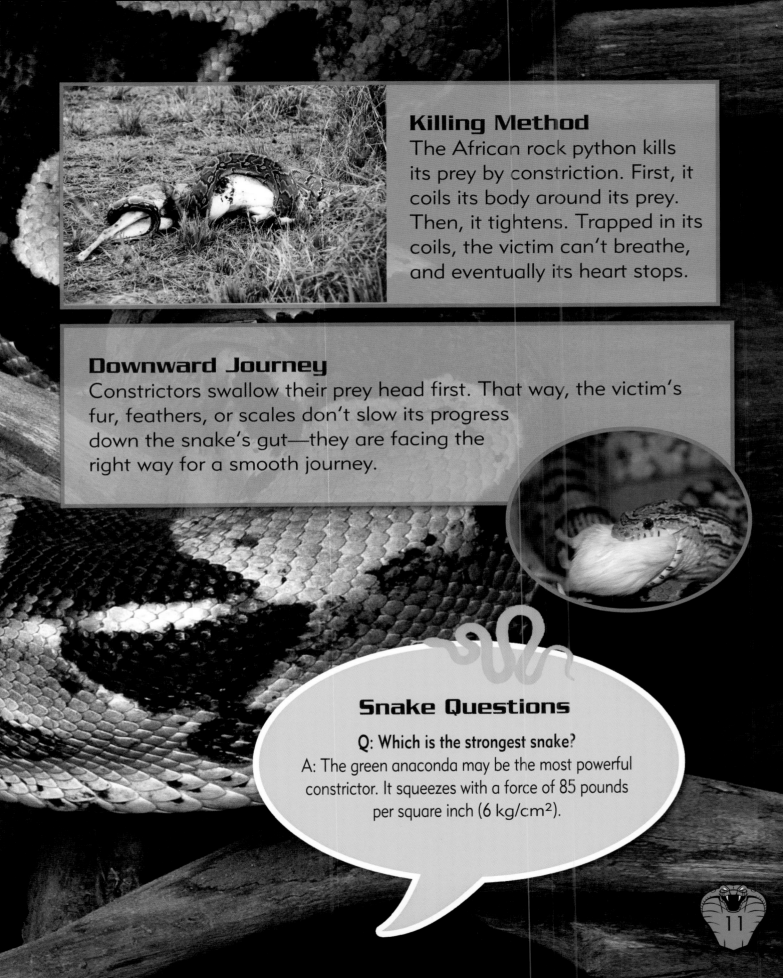

Killing Method

The African rock python kills its prey by constriction. First, it coils its body around its prey. Then, it tightens. Trapped in its coils, the victim can't breathe, and eventually its heart stops.

Downward Journey

Constrictors swallow their prey head first. That way, the victim's fur, feathers, or scales don't slow its progress down the snake's gut—they are facing the right way for a smooth journey.

Snake Questions

Q: Which is the strongest snake?
A: The green anaconda may be the most powerful constrictor. It squeezes with a force of 85 pounds per square inch (6 kg/cm²).

Venomous Snakes

If you were a venomous snake (like the rattlesnake shown right), you would use a poisonous liquid called venom to kill or stun your prey. You would have two long, sharp fangs for injecting the venom.

Spitting Cobras

Some snakes use venom for defense as well as attack. If a predator comes within 10 feet (3 m) of a spitting cobra, it may be sprayed with venom. The venom squirts from the cobra's fangs. If it gets in an attacker's eyes, it can cause blindness.

Fearsome Fangs

When a venomous snake strikes, it sinks its fangs into its prey. Like a pair of deadly syringes, they pump venom into the victim's flesh. Vipers' fangs are so long that they have to fold back flat when they're not being used.

Record-breakers

Belcher's sea snake (below right) is the world's most venomous snake. Just one bite contains enough venom to kill 1,000 people. That's 10 times stronger than the most venomous land snake, the inland taipan. This shy, brown snake lives in dry central Australia.

Snake Questions

Q: What should I do if I'm bitten by a snake?
A: Snake bites can cause breathing difficulties, paralysis, hemorrhaging, and even death. Tell a doctor what's bitten you—show a photo if you can—so that you can be given the right antivenin as soon as possible.

Feeding

If you were a snake, your meals might be rodents, frogs, lizards, birds, or even other snakes. If you were a really large snake, you might feast on much larger prey, such as gazelles, zebras, or crocodiles.

Giant Gape

Snakes are able to swallow big prey whole because their lower jaw comes loose. Snakes use their backward-facing teeth to pull prey into the mouth and push it down the throat. Then, muscles move the meal along their stretchy-skinned body.

Food Processing

A snake might take a week or more to digest a large meal. The work of breaking down the food can make the snake's heart swell by 40 percent and its liver double in size. Afterward, the snake may not need to eat again for months.

A Diet of Eggs

Egg-eating snakes raid birds' nests for their meals. First, the egg-eater crams the egg into its toothless mouth. Next, spines inside its throat pierce the egg, and the snake swallows its contents. Finally, the snake spits out the empty shell.

Snake Questions

Q: Do snakes drink?
A: Yes, they drink water. Some suck it up as if they are drinking through a straw. Others use folds in their jaw to soak up the liquid like a sponge.

How Snakes Move

If you were a snake, you'd be unlike many land animals because you wouldn't have any legs. You'd still manage to move around, though. If you were the speediest snake, the black mamba, you could dash at up to 12 mph (20 km/h)— faster than the average person can run!

Serpentine Movement

Most of the time, snakes move forward by "undulating" their body— squeezing their muscles so their body weaves along in a series of S-bends. In a tight space, a snake bunches up its whole body into a concertina shape and then pushes forward.

Snake Questions

Q: Did snakes ever have legs?
A: Snakes evolved long ago from a four-legged, lizardlike reptile. Early snakes burrowed or swam, and legs got in the way. So, over many generations, snakes lost their legs. To this day, pythons still have a pair of clawlike "spurs"—the remains of their hind legs.

Good Grips

On ordinary terrain, snakes rely on the rough edges of their ventral (underside) scales to give them grip. But in deserts, the sand is often loose and hot. Some desert snakes have developed a clever sidewinding technique, so that very little of their body touches the sand.

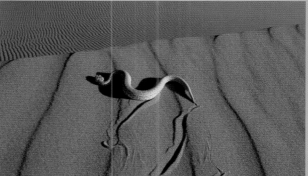

The Flying Snake

The paradise flying snake lives in rain forests. It cannot really fly like a bird, but it can glide up to 33 feet (100 m) from tree to tree. It sucks in its underside and stretches out its ribs, shaping its body like a simple wing.

Swimming Snakes

If you were a snake, you might live in the sea, or perhaps a lake or lagoon. In that case, you would feed on fish or crustaceans. You would probably have a small head and neck, allowing you to reach deep into holes and crevices in underwater rocks and coral.

Sea-Living Snakes

Two different families of snakes have adapted to life at sea—sea snakes (main image) and sea kraits (near right). Both have paddlelike tails and can breathe in air through the top of their skin. They can usually stay underwater for around half an hour.

Life Underwater

Most sea-living snakes stick to the shallows and coastal waters, such as coral reefs. Different species have different diets— some hunt for eels, some catch crabs, and some scrape fish eggs off underwater rocks. Many have powerful venom to paralyze their prey.

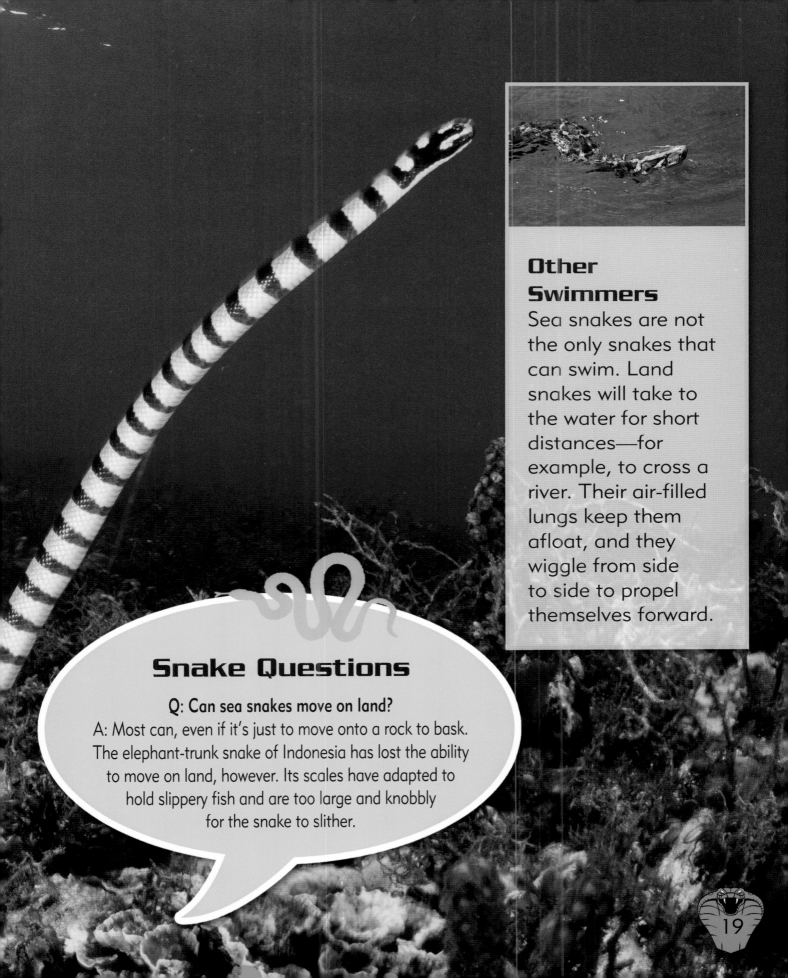

Other Swimmers

Sea snakes are not the only snakes that can swim. Land snakes will take to the water for short distances—for example, to cross a river. Their air-filled lungs keep them afloat, and they wiggle from side to side to propel themselves forward.

Snake Questions

Q: Can sea snakes move on land?
A: Most can, even if it's just to move onto a rock to bask. The elephant-trunk snake of Indonesia has lost the ability to move on land, however. Its scales have adapted to hold slippery fish and are too large and knobbly for the snake to slither.

Snake Talk

If you were a snake, you would probably be a solitary creature. You would spend a lot of your life lying in wait for prey and would rarely need to communicate with other animals. You'd use sounds to warn off occasional attackers and chemicals to send messages to fellow snakes.

Hiss, Hiss

Most snakes hiss when they are disturbed—it's their way of warning a predator that they will bite back. Even nonvenomous snakes can give a rather painful bite, thanks to long, curved fangs.

Warning Noise

Rattlesnakes are named for the unusual rattling sound they make to frighten off bigger animals. The "rattle" at the end of their tail is made up of hardened pieces of old scales that clatter together when the snake shakes its tail.

Talking to Each Other

Snakes communicate with each other using pheromones—special chemicals produced by the body. A female will give off these chemicals when she is ready to mate, and this is how nearby males are able to track her down.

Snake Questions

Q: How far away can a rattlesnake be heard?
A: The noise travels about 33 feet (10 m). Each time the snake sheds its skin, the rattle gets bigger (and louder), but every so often, the oldest part of the rattle breaks off, so it becomes quieter again.

Snake Defenses

If you were a snake, you would have cunning ways to attack others, and you'd have sneaky tricks for defending and protecting yourself. One technique that you might use to get rid of predators would be to lie on your back and simply play dead!

Confusing Colors

Deadly snakes are often colorful, as a warning to predators to leave them alone. The coral snake, for instance, is red and black. So is the milk snake (shown here)—but it's all a con! Milk snakes are harmless, but attackers steer clear of them because they look like coral snakes.

Looking Fierce

Many snakes try to keep attackers away by looking bigger than they really are. The champion is the cobra, which spreads out its hood when threatened. Cobras prefer to scare away a threat rather than waste valuable venom on fighting it off.

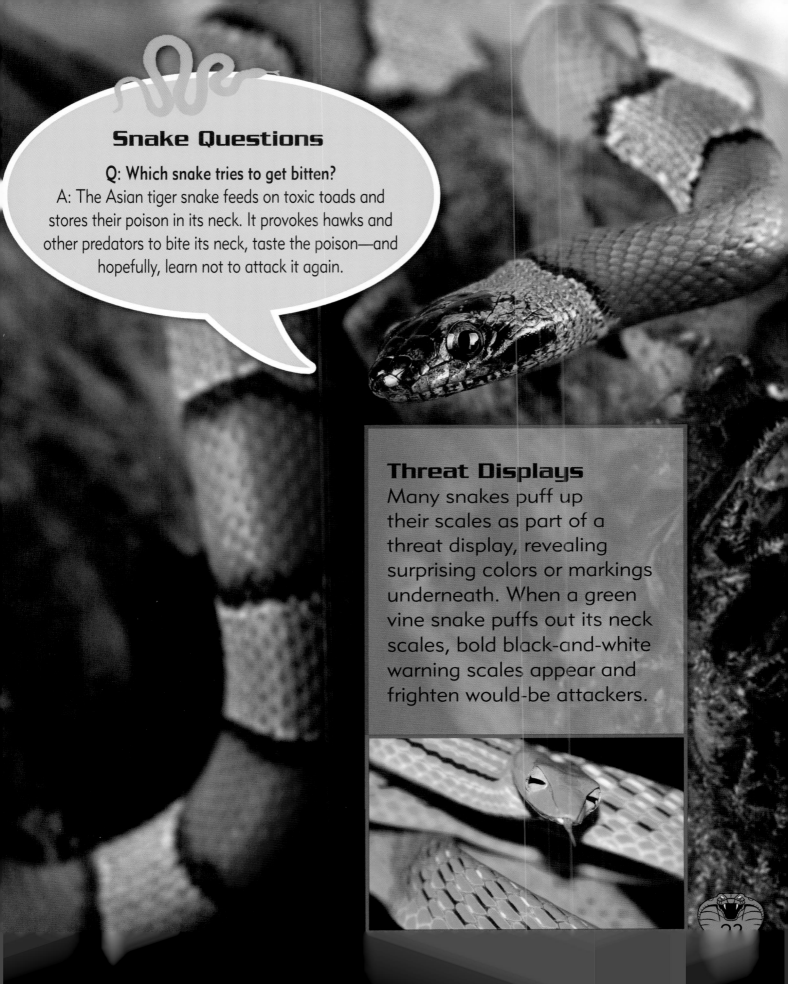

Snake Questions

Q: Which snake tries to get bitten?
A: The Asian tiger snake feeds on toxic toads and stores their poison in its neck. It provokes hawks and other predators to bite its neck, taste the poison—and hopefully, learn not to attack it again.

Threat Displays

Many snakes puff up their scales as part of a threat display, revealing surprising colors or markings underneath. When a green vine snake puffs out its neck scales, bold black-and-white warning scales appear and frighten would-be attackers.

Snake Skin

If you were a snake, your long, limbless body would be covered in scaly snakeskin. As you grew, you'd become too big for your skin and need to molt, or shed it. Unlike humans, who lose old skin cells each day, you would shed your entire skin at one time.

What Snakes Feel Like

The gloss and shine of a snake's scales can make it look slimy—especially to people who are scared of snakes. In reality, if you are lucky enough to touch a snake, you will find that its skin feels dry, smooth, and cool.

Scales and Skin

A snake's skin is made up of tiny, transparent overlapping scales that sit on a stretchy thin skin. The scales form a flexible suit of armor that protects the whole body—there are even scales over the snake's eyes.

Snake Questions

Q: Do any other animals shed their skin?
A: Yes, lizards do. Like snakes, they're reptiles. Not all reptiles shed their skin, though—crocodiles and turtles don't.

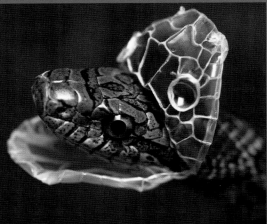

Shedding

When a snake sheds its skin, it usually comes off in one snake-shaped piece. The skin splits at the lip, and the snake may rub itself against rough objects to help ease the skin off. A brand-new shiny skin is waiting underneath.

Baby Snakes

If you were a snake, you would have begun life in one of two ways. Your mother might have given birth to you, or you might have hatched out of an egg. Depending on your species, you might have been your mom's only baby—or one of a hundred or more!

Egg-Layers

Most snakes lay eggs—soft, leathery ones—and then leave them. Cobras stick around to guard the clutch, however, and pythons even keep the eggs warm. When the babies are ready to hatch, they break the eggshell with a special "egg tooth" on their snout that drops off as soon as its job is done.

Live Young

Boa constrictor, garter snake, and rattlesnake moms don't lay eggs—they keep the fertilized eggs inside their bodies as the babies develop. Then, they give birth to live young that usually look just like miniature adults.

Snake Questions

Q: What do baby snakes eat?
A: Hatchlings eat live prey, just as adults do. Because of their size, they usually tackle smaller animals, such as mice, lizards, or frogs.

Changing Color

Sometimes snake babies don't look like their parents—they are a different color. Newborn emerald tree boas (shown on the right) start life yellow or red and then turn green when they are a year old.

Where Snakes Live

If you were a snake, you might live almost anywhere in the world. Your scaly skin would keep in water, allowing you to survive in dry, desert regions. You would be ectothermic (unable to produce your own body heat), so you would not be able to live anywhere very cold.

Keeping a Steady Temperature

Snakes heat up by basking in the sun and cool down by finding a shady spot or by burrowing. Most land snakes live in hot or warm parts of the world, where the climate does not change much all year round.

Surviving Cold

Snakes that do live in colder parts of the world have found their own ways to survive. Garter snakes, for instance, spend the colder winter months sleeping ("brumating"). They shut down their body systems and do not need to eat until spring.

Home, Sweet Home

Most snakes do not really make their own homes. Those that live in forests hang out in trees or lurk among the leaf litter. In harsher environments, snakes might seek shelter in a rocky crevice or an abandoned burrow.

Snake Questions

Q: Are snakes found everywhere?
A: No, they're not. After the last Ice Age, no snakes survived in Antarctica, Greenland, Iceland, New Zealand, or Ireland. According to legend, a holy man named St. Patrick banished the snakes from Ireland.

Glossary

ambush To carry out a surprise attack.

antivenin Medicine used to treat someone who has been bitten by a snake and reverse the effects of the venom.

bask To lie in the sun to warm up.

brumating Having a winter sleep. Reptiles and amphibians brumate to survive the coldest parts of the year, just as some mammals hibernate.

caiman A small member of the crocodile family that lives in Central and South America.

camouflage Markings or coloring that blend in to the surroundings and make an animal hard to spot.

capybara A pig-sized South American rodent.

climate The average weather of a place over the year.

constriction Killing by squeezing an animal so tightly that its heart stops.

crustacean An animal with a shell. Crabs, lobsters, and barnacles are all crustaceans.

digest To break down food.

ectothermic Unable to produce body heat and relying on the outside environment, especially the sun, for warmth.

egg tooth A special tooth that helps a baby snake to hatch and then drops off.

evolved Changed very slowly over time.

heat pit A heat-sensitive pit, or opening, on a snake's face that can detect tiny changes in temperature, such as extra heat coming from the body of warm-blooded prey. All pit vipers have heat pits and so do some boas and pythons.

hemorrhaging Losing blood. This can happen internally, when blood leaks inside the body, or outside through a wound.

Jacobsen's organ A sense organ that detects chemicals and scents.

kg/cm² Kilograms per square centimeter, a measurement of force.

lagoon An enclosed area of sea.

leaf litter The layer of fallen and decaying leaves on a forest floor.

luring Attracting or tempting to come near.

molt To lose or shed skin. Older snakes may only shed their skin once or twice a year; young ones may molt once every two weeks.

paralysis Not being able to move.

paralyze Make something unable to move.

receptor A part of the body that can sense or receive information.

serpentine Snakelike, or S-shaped.

sidewinding A way of moving by repeatedly throwing the body to the side in a loop.

solitary Alone.

terrain Ground or land.

thermogram A "heat picture" that shows the relative temperatures of something, for instance, shading cooler areas blue and warmer areas red.

toxic Poisonous.

undulating Moving up and down.

ventral scale Any of the scales on the underside of a snake.

Further Reading

100 Facts: Snakes by Barbara Taylor (Miles Kelly Publishing, 2010)

Amazing Animals: Snakes by Jen Green (W.B. Saunders Company, 2012)

Really Weird Animals: Snakes and Lizards by Clare Hibbert (Arcturus, 2011)

Snake by Chris Mattison (Dorling Kindersley, 2006)

Snakes and Other Reptiles by Andrew Solway (Heinemann Library, 2007)

Usborne Discovery: Snakes by Rachel Firth and Jonathan Sheikh-Miller (Usborne, 2010)

Web Sites

animals.nationalgeographic.com/animals/photos/snakes/
A photo gallery of snakes from around the world.

http://animals.howstuffworks.com/reptiles
Animal Planet's guide to reptiles including amazing snake videos.

www.pitt.edu/~mcs2/herp/SoNA.html
An online database that lists the snakes of North America.

www.snakeconservation.org
The web site of the Center for Snake Conservation, a nonprofit organization.

www.tpt.org/newtons/video_only.php?id=2036
A short video about rain forest snakes.

Index